5 Steps to Surviving Teaching: Tips for Conquering the First Year and Every Year

By Julie C. Gilbert

Aletheia Pyralis Publishers

For information about special discounts available for bulk purchases, sales promotions, fund-raising and educational needs, please email: juliecgilbert5steps@gmail.com.

Keep up with news and giveaways by joining my Nonfiction Newsletter: http://www.juliecgilbert.com/ - see this site to grab some free biology and chemistry projects https://sites.google.com/view/juliecgilbert-writer/

Love Science Fiction or Mystery?

Dedication:

To the many teachers whose experiences shaped me or this book.

Table of Contents:

Introduction:

Dear Teacher or Teacher-to-Be:

You may be wondering ...

Who is this book for?
Whether you're in a teaching program, in the midst of your first year, or well on your way to burnout, I hope you can draw inspiration from this book. I am a science teacher, so it will have a lot of information applicable to lab portions of the class that might not apply to everybody. Still, I hope it's useful to you.

What is this book and what is it not?
What follows will be a collection of my thoughts and reflections on the teaching profession. Some people may frown upon the lack of statistics and hard research. Over the years, I've become slightly disenchanted with the teaching fads and buzz words. This will be a down-in-the-trenches sort of first-hand look at education in suburban America, specifically in my home state of New Jersey.

A friend recently gave me a rundown on public education in England. While the specifics of the system may differ, people are still people, so the take-away lessons should still be applicable regardless of where in the world you teach.

It is not a textbook, nor is it solely a how-to manual, though I will share some tips and tricks I've learned over the years. Since it's based on my personal experiences, it doesn't address teaching in an urban or rural setting or in a boarding school.

Who the heck are you and why are you writing about teaching?

I'm a writer, and I'm a teacher. After more than a decade writing and almost a decade teaching, I figured I might as well stop fighting the inevitable and just write a book about my teaching experiences. I've been meaning to write a book about teaching for a few years, but lacked the time, content, and collective drive to just sit down and do it. But I seem to be on a nonfiction kick right now. Strike while the iron's hot and so forth. I'm interested to see where it goes because the book that would have been written a few years ago is definitely not the same one that will be formed now, and if I wait another few months or years, the story will change again.

More specifically, I'm a high school chemistry teacher, but I've also done a year of biology and taught fifth grade science. I've also taught in both public and private school settings.

How is this book laid out?

First up, you'll hear a bit more about me so you understand where I'm coming from. Next, I'll comment on some myths and misconceptions about the teaching profession. That should be fun. Then, I'll dive into the heart of what you need to survive as a teacher. That part might encompass quite a few chapters. If you really want to get to the "save me, I'm drowning" part, go to chapter five. Finally, I'll lay out some questions and comments to help you decide if you're all-in or in over your head.

Legal Boringness:

For legal reasons, I will only generally reference students or former colleagues. I will also change the names as necessary.

This isn't about targeting anybody. It's about pointing out some of the things I've learned along my rather varied teaching career.

5 Steps to Mastering the First Year:
Step 1: Gain good perspective and define why you do what you do
Step 2: Plan at least two to three weeks ahead
Step 3: Manage your "me time"
Step 4: Pick your battles and press on
Step 5: Communicate with parents, students, and colleagues regularly
Bonus: Do what you love, love what you do

5 Steps to Mastering the First Year (the annotated version...)
Step 1: Gain good perspective and define why you do what you do
Why did you become a teacher? Or why do you want to become a teacher? What do you seek to gain from the profession? If you just want to pay your bills, there are probably easier ways of doing so. If you want to make a difference in young people's lives, that's great and noble, but it's not enough on its own. If you simply love the subject you teach, that's awesome too, but again, alone it's not enough to justify all the junk you're going to encounter in the career.

You don't have to write down eight goals you'd like to accomplish in the next ten years, but it's not a completely rubbish idea to know who you are, where you came from, and where you're going.

The second half of this step might sound mystical, but it's not. Sticking with teaching's going to have you writing a whole heap of objectives throughout your career, you might as well add a few more to your list. What makes you uniquely qualified to teach these students for 40-minutes to an hour most days of the year for nine months?

Step 2: Plan at least two to three weeks ahead

I actually don't recommend going too much further ahead than two to three weeks, but there are always exceptions. Some of my colleagues go four to six weeks ahead and that works for them. I've found that things change. Short notice assemblies have a way of randomly taking out part of your classes. That's right. Part. Assemblies rarely last the whole day and often go by grade level, so you could find yourself missing half of first period one day and half of third period on a different day. Occasionally, you get a lot of notice on an assembly, but then, by the time it rolls around, you've forgotten about it and need to make adjustments anyway.

Flexibility. I'm not a fan of the word or what it stands for, but it's necessary.

Staying two weeks ahead gives you some leeway when unexpected things pop up in your life. I've observed that teachers come in two main flavors: those that are there all the time and those that are hardly there. Every school and every program's going to have different requirements for how you write your lesson plans, but regardless of the format, they should be understood by pretty much everybody reading them.

Step 3: Manage your "me time"

You might have to schedule in time for you and your family. Truth is, with a job like this, there's literally always more you could be doing. So, you need to be purposeful about doing other things you love. Whether that's exercising, reading, watching TV, going to movies, or just playing with your kids, the "me time" will keep you sane.

American culture values hard work, which is good, but there's more to life than your job. If you don't find time to rest and recharge, you won't be able to teach to your maximum capacity.

It's not hard physical labor, but it is surprisingly demanding on your body. You can expect to be on your feet for much of the day. Think about it, this is one of the few professions where you have to schedule what times you can use the restroom because the other option is leave twenty-five children or teenagers unsupervised. Depending on your school, you can usually find somebody from hall duty or the main office to cover for you in an emergency, but the point remains: planning is important.

Step 4: Pick your battles and press on
Conflict and judgment calls will crop up regularly. Whether it's a dispute with a student over whether or not they handed in an assignment on time or a parent questioning how you graded something, you're going to have to learn which battles to fight and which to let go. Defining your grading policy early on helps, but every situation is unique.

Hard truth: Many parents feel very free about questioning you, your policies, and your qualifications if their kid earns anything less than an A. This is not a retail situation; the "customer" is not always right. They do occasionally bring up valid points, and you should always consider their point of view. However, be VERY cautious about changing grades to suit their whims. It's a slippery slope. If you yield even once, you will open yourself to a whole lot more of people questioning you.

Parents seem to have the notion that hard work should equate to top marks. I've been asked to change a final grade from an 89 to a 90 based on a student's work ethic. That's definitely the sort of situation where I recommend standing your ground. Otherwise, the grading system means zip and you might as well go back to handing out cards and letting people fill in the grade they'd like to receive.

As for the dispute over whether or not a student handed in an assignment, I generally go for the compromise. Tell the student to search their things while you search your papers. Most of the time, they'll find the assignment. If neither of you can find it, let the student re-do the assignment free of a late penalty. They might be annoyed, but if they've done it once they should have no problem repeating the work.

If there's a dispute over when an assignment was turned in, give them the benefit of the doubt. It will build rapport and in the end won't affect their grade much either way.

Cell phones: Either find a way to utilize them for good or shut them down quickly. Be consistent. Be fair. Be firm.

Step 5: Communicate with parents, students, and colleagues regularly

This past year, I decided to write the students and the parents a weekly email update. It took about an hour each Saturday or Sunday, but I think it was worthwhile. Most parents liked seeing what their students were up to in class. The emails also gave me the opportunity to put in reminders of when major assignments were due or when the students should come prepared for lab.

To be honest, I don't know how many students read the weekly email. Next year, I'd like to put in something to make it slightly interactive, so I can gauge how often it's being used. Nevertheless, a weekly email to students is good because it keeps the website fresh and it takes away some excuses they could make about being unprepared.

Bonus: Do what you love, love what you do

There will be good days and bad days. Take a moment to think about what made the good days awesome and what made the bad days horrible. If at the end of the year you can say you still love what you do, then you should stick with it.

Embrace Your Destiny ...

Or at least find a place that fits you. I've worked in several different places. If one type of school doesn't work out for you, there are plenty of others to consider. Urban, suburban, rural, and private schools offer a wide range of vastly different experiences. Also, each school has pros and cons. The problems you face will change year to year and place to place, but in the end, kids still need great teachers in every subject.

Conclusion:

Congratulations. You've chosen a highly satisfying, crazy challenging, moderately compensated career.

If you have comments or questions, you can always email me at juliecgilbert5steps@gmail.com. Please do me a favor and put "Teaching" somewhere in the subject to help me distinguish which 5 Steps book you're referring to. Keep up with news and giveaways by joining my nonfiction newsletter: http://www.juliecgilbert.com/ (See website for most updated link.)

Sincerely,

Julie C. Gilbert
Chemistry Teacher

Chapter 1:
Four First-Year Experiences

Introduction:

Some people might read that and think "wow, you really stink at this" while others will see it as "wow, what a lot of experience you have to share." Keep in mind, everybody's path will be different. A few people start out in a different career and end up picking up teaching later in life as a second career. Others know what they want to be from the time they're old enough to read. There's no right or wrong way to get into the profession, but in order to become a certified teacher, you have to be pretty purposeful about it because there are quite a few hoops to jump through. I'll expand a bit on that later.

The First Year of First-Year Teaching:

Since I graduated with an undergrad degree in biology, naturally, that's the subject I taught first upon finishing my Masters of Arts in Teaching. The actual first-year teaching experience is probably going to be one of the hardest, most emotionally challenging parts of your career. If you can make it through that, you can do almost anything.

Right out of the grad program, I found a job teaching at a suburban public school about twenty-five minutes from home. Some of the kids came across as snotty, my boss was new to supervising, and I had absolutely no clue what I was doing. Bad combination. The school gave me a mentor who wasn't even teaching the same subject. To put it mildly, things didn't work out well. They didn't renew the contract, and I was more than ready to quit the profession altogether. However, things worked out such that I ended up getting a new job at the private high school I'd attended.

The Second Year of First-Year Teaching:

I taught chemistry a total of four years at my old high school, and that's where I learned to love teaching. Two years into that four-year tenure, I had the urge to return to college so I could get the formal certification to teach chemistry everywhere in the state. When the school fell upon tough financial times, I took the opportunity to do just that. I re-enrolled at The College of New Jersey as a non-matriculated student and did a semester of three chemistry courses and a statistics course.

Upon finishing that, I took the Chemistry Praxis and filed for the second standard license. That disastrous year of teaching biology in a public school made the process of getting the second license very easy. A few months later, I took a job at a high school about fifteen minutes away from home.

The Third Year of First-Year Teaching:

I guess you could say this was a year-and-a-half in length because I came on in April of the year I completed the chemistry license. Coming in mid-year added new challenges. By the time I reached my second full year there, I'd made some good friends and was comfortable. Perhaps too comfortable. So, imagine my surprise when they too chose not to renew the contract. I think they were afraid I couldn't adapt to the Next Generation Science Standards.

Back to rethinking my life. In hindsight, the move forced a change in me for the better. I found a new job teaching at a school in North Jersey, got an apartment, and moved.

9

The Fourth Year of First-Year Teaching:

A new suburban school to me, but this time, there were several distinct differences, including the change to a block schedule. I'll chat about types of schedules later. There are so many different ways to write schedules.

Took me four tries, but I found a good fit. It's a regional school but about half the size of my previous school. The hour-long blocks give teachers a decent chance to dive into a significant chunk of material without dragging on too long. The administration tends to be supportive on discipline issues. The science department works decently well together. The students are generally good-natured, and I like the people I work with. These might seem like small things, but let any one of them be difficult and watch the threads of your sanity fray.

Conclusion:

Don't let one or two bad experiences limit you.

My experience will not be the same as yours, but if you consider the things I've learned along the way, perhaps you can find your way quicker than I did. There are hundreds and thousands of schools both public and private, local and far from home, so keep an open mind when the going gets rough.

Chapter 2:
Anybody Can Teach … Sort of

First Myth about Teachers:

Anybody can do it. This statement is true if you go with the broadest definition of simply passing on knowledge. But not everybody can be a public or private, primary or secondary school teacher. We could go on numerous bunny trails here exploring the exceptions to this, such as adult schools and other alternative schools. For simplicity, we'll stick with a narrow definition.

There are some basic requirements for becoming a certified public school teacher in the state of New Jersey. All states have similar requirements, and I'm pretty sure all countries have comparable requirements. Within the United States, once you have a certification there is a system for reciprocity, meaning you can obtain a certification in a different state with minimal trouble. The only one that seemed more annoying to try and get was New York.

Basic Requirements:

To become certified, you need a Bachelor's degree. You'll also need thirty college credits in the subject you'd like to teach. I mention that because my Bachelor's degree is for Biology but

I'm dual certified to teach both biology and chemistry. However, I went back to college to get the rest of the chemistry credits. I didn't graduate college with enough. You also need to pass the Praxis exams. Some certifications have multiple tests. For example, the chemistry one required a Chemistry specific Praxis as well as the General Science Praxis. Incidentally, you can't have a criminal record, which I think is a reasonable requirement.

Private schools can make up their own rules for teacher candidate requirements, but I'm fairly certain most still hold with the "lack of a criminal record" thing. Some private schools may even have additional requirements based on faith and other shared beliefs.

What makes a good teacher?

When you look for a teaching job, you can expect to be asked what you think makes a good teacher. Do some thinking on this ahead of time. Why do you want to be a teacher? If you're in it for the money, definitely wrong career path.

While there is no personality requirement for becoming a teacher, there are some general traits that could help. A passion for young people and the subject you teach are both a must in my humble opinion. Patience, kindness, selflessness, dedication, self-motivation, humility, a sense of humor, ingenuity, and high organization skills are important too.

Passion and People:

Did you know some people grow up playing school teacher? One of my former colleagues said she used to ask her elementary teacher for some papers she could pretend were homework assignments. Passion of that sort for the profession may not be a strict requirement, but it certainly can't hurt.

I decided to become a teacher during my senior year of college because by then I knew research wasn't for me, yet I still loved biology. It made sense to pick up a profession that allowed me to explore the subject I love at the level I learned to love it: high school. I'll readily admit that a passion for the subject initially brought me to the teaching profession, but I think if you don't develop a desire to connect with students, it's a tough career to stick with.

A Giving Spirit and Understanding Nature:

I'm going to lump kindness, selflessness, and dedication into one commentary about having a giving spirit. Many aspects of teaching are tedious and thankless. Talking about money usually makes people mad, but I'm going to risk it for the sake of thoroughness. If you surveyed a hundred teachers, I'd bet you a dollar that each and every one of them has at some point in their career bought something for their classroom, whether that be colored pencils, glue, stickers, a PowerPoint clicker, calculators, or food coloring. Most schools have funds for basic school supplies, but sometimes you need something right now. These supplies you purchase out of pocket are tax deductible, which is nice, but the fact remains that a giving spirit makes one a better fit for the job.

Content Knowledge:

You need to know your subject, but be prepared to learn new things about the subject. The best way to learn something is to teach it. You need to know enough in order to be able to answer questions that arise during class discussions.

Humility:

Humility is at the core of a willingness to learn. As a teacher, you'll be called upon to learn a lot both about the subject and about people. There are times when you'll have to admit that you don't know an answer, but if you tell somebody you'll get back to them, follow through. Kids are very sharp when it comes to score keeping. Admitting you don't know but then going a step beyond to find the answers they seek will go a long way in earning their trust.

Good Sense of Humor:

A good sense of humor is a vital life skill in any job, especially teaching. I have a very dry sense of humor, and I have a tendency toward mild sarcasm. The majority of high school students will connect well with such an approach, though I must caution I've run across one or two who have no sense for it and will be easily offended. In such cases, perhaps a different approach will be necessary. If you are genuine, most students will reciprocate. Don't be afraid to laugh at yourself if the situation arises. There's a fine line between self-respect and arrogance. I never agreed with the old adage to not smile at the students until mid-year. Laughter is good for everybody. The more you can show the kids you love doing what you do, the better chance you have of convincing them your class might not be the worst thing that ever struck them or their GPA.

Adaptability:

Be inventive and be prepared to adapt on the fly. Don't let little things throw you off. Expect technology troubles and have a backup plan that relies on simpler things like pen and paper or a chalkboard.

Organization Skills:

I'm told that some teachers are highly disorganized. I guess it could happen, but my experience has mostly been with science teachers. By and large, we're a fairly organized lot. This isn't the make or break attribute, but it helps if you can keep track of a large number of goings-on. Classrooms can be chaos. Try to keep it organized chaos. If you think you're going to march into a modern high school classroom and lecture for fifty minutes, you have a very big reality check coming. Turning more of the learning over to students means that more of the battle shifts to keeping them on-task.

Love:

Always remember to do what you love and love what you do. I'm not talking about a fickle or casual love, but a deep, dedicated sort where you're willing to sacrifice a lot to keep it.

Conclusion:

This list is not comprehensive, but it's a good start.

Chapter 3:
Comments on Twenty Teaching Myths

Introduction:
Since I'm not about to split hairs over what's a myth and what's a misconception, this list will include a random assortment of both. The link to the original websites I found most of them at is below if you'd like to read what other people have to say.

Myth #1: Those who can't do, teach.
Not even sure how this one got started. In order to teach something, you need to have a better understanding of the skill or subject. Coaching's a form of teaching, and most coaches have some experience with the sport they're passing on, even if it's not at the professional level.

Teaching's not as glamorous as being a movie star, a rocket scientist, a doctor, or a lawyer, but its effects as a profession are further reaching. Every movie star, rocket scientist, doctor, and lawyer in modern society had interactions with an ordinary or extraordinary teacher once upon a time. Some geniuses had bad experiences with their teachers, but on the whole, those who teach do so because it's a passion and a calling.

Myth #2: Teachers get out so early each day. (3:00 p.m.)

While technically true, this is one of the few professions where you're expected to do a lot of work outside of "normal" hours. Papers don't grade themselves, though there are companies you can hire if you really want to outsource your grading duties. Not sure how that works because there's always a lot of judgment calls when it comes to grading. Lessons don't just magically appear either. I spend nearly every Saturday working through lesson plans. Nobody pays you overtime or says "well done" when you spend nights and weekends doing work for school. That's just part of the job.

Myth #3 and #4: Teachers get three months off in the summer, and their vacations are paid.

Year-round schools are becoming more popular, but the majority of schools still have summer. Still, it's not exactly three months. It's about two months in length and you don't get paid. You can choose to have your ten-month salary spread over twelve months if you'd like, but that simply means you get less each paycheck. It's not being paid for a vacation. It's you choosing to budget for the summer months.

Myth #5: Teachers sit behind a desk all day.

There might be a time when you get to sit at your desk, but mostly, you'll be walking around interacting with the students. Try controlling the behavior of twenty to twenty-five students from behind a desk. It doesn't work very well.

Myth #6: Teachers don't have to plan.

I guess it could happen, but students are going to know you're unprepared and tune you out pretty quickly. The best policy is to over plan because the quickest road to chaos involves bored teenagers. There are times you'll have to adapt your plan in the moment, but it's never the best practice. Careful planning's pretty much a cornerstone to running a smooth classroom.

Myth #7: Teachers can do everything.

Pretty sure some administrators I've worked for believe this whole-heartedly. While a nice sentiment, it's not true. Teachers are pretty adaptable as a species, but they can't do everything well. Teachers may temporarily take on the role of hand-writing analysis expert, disciplinarian, or moderator, but we have our limits.

Myth #8: Teaching is easy.

Certain parts of teaching are easy, fun, and enjoyable, but it's still hard work. The training involved in becoming a teacher might not be as rigorous as some other fields, but there's a lot you learn on the job. Like any job, it's emotionally rewarding but also challenging and taxing. Your feet will hurt, and your heart will ache at times.

Further musings: There aren't always life and death situations, but you also have no idea how much the young people sitting in your classroom will retain. Students learn way more than the subject content in school. They learn how to interact with others, work in groups, meet deadlines, and do hard things. Like it or not, they will watch you and judge you for what you do or fail to do.

Classrooms are benevolent dictatorships. Nobody will thank you if you let the students do whatever they want. You need to establish order, fair play, and rules to keep the peace. As long as they see value in it, students tend to want to complete the work you set out for them. Balancing added value, perceived value, and state requirements is doable but definitely not easy.

Myth #9: Teachers don't get sick because they build up a tolerance for germs.

Before the last week of the 2016-2017 school year, I might have agreed with this, but then I spent about three weeks running a high fever, coughing, and generally feeling miserable.

Myth #10: Teachers — especially elementary school teachers — play with students all day.

While you can have fun teaching, there's still work getting done. At certain grades, play might be part of the social order of the day, and society as a whole benefits when children learn to share, get along, and play nicely. But they also learn to read, write, and do math.

Myth #11: Teachers are overpaid.

You can earn a decent wage being a teacher, but it's certainly not a get-rich-quick scheme. Most first-year teaching jobs I've seen in New Jersey ranged from low $40,000 to low $50,000. You hear about teachers who earn $80,000 or $90,000, but generally, that's because they've been working for thirty years.

Private schools can be all over the salary map. My experience with private schools has been that they pay about half of what I can make in a public school, but remember that my experience is only at one school. Schools are privately run for many different reasons, and many do offer wages closer to public school scales.

Myth #12: There are always a lot of teaching jobs available.

That depends on what you teach and where you're willing to teach. Sure, there are always jobs available, but like any profession, the fit of the jobs available will vary. Is the job close enough to home or do you have to move? Does it pay enough to support you and your family?

If you teach high school physics, you probably have a lot more options about where to go and what you make. It seems like there are a lot more biology candidates for each position. Chemistry's sort of in the middle of physics and biology in terms of being in demand. As far as I know, English and Social Studies vary, but I think the field is still strong for math teachers.

There tend to be more openings in places where it is harder to find viable candidates, such as rural or urban districts. For some reason, I keep hearing that Hawaii's in constant demand for teachers. I believe private boarding schools pay pretty well, but those jobs can be scarce because there aren't that many of them compared to other types of schools.

Myth #13: Teachers have a lot of free time each day.

Free time can vary day-to-day. At my current school, one day I can have two periods off or with a low maintenance duty and the next I'll work five periods in a row. I've learned to do a lot of grading during the school day, but it's been almost a decade and I still can't concentrate well enough to lesson plan mid-day.

Myth #14: Students are well-behaved.

The majority of students are well-mannered and well-behaved, but it really only takes two or three knuckleheads to make the whole balance tip to chaos. Students are people too. They have good days and bad days. Their moods can be volatile but less so as they get older and their impulse control grows. (Hopefully.)

There's a direct link between classroom management and student behavior. While you as the teacher can't control everything, the better you handle the class, the more well-behaved students will be. I'll admit that certain classrooms are much easier to control than others. Every year's different.

Myth #15: Students get things the first time you teach them.

Ha. Get ready to repeat yourself a lot. People don't always hear you the first time, even those genuinely interested in following the instructions. At other times, you will be fighting the fact that they're five, six, or fifteen and fidgety by nature. Patience is a virtue you'll either have to possess or fake very well. With time, you'll develop "The Look" which will alert the students to pay closer attention to what will soon be said, but verbal cues are also necessary.

Myth #16: Teachers don't have to pay for their own supplies.

I saw a meme once that said something like "Teaching's the one profession where you steal supplies from home and take them to work." That pretty much sums up the answer to this one. It's hard to say how much I spend every year on supplies. As a chemistry teacher, I'm usually scouring grocery stores for baking soda, vinegar, food coloring, sugar, paper plates, plastic spoons, plastic cups, or distilled water. Schools supply textbooks, dry erase markers, chalk, and white out. They even spring for stock chemicals, but they typically don't do lab supplies that can be bought at most stores. Certain schools might have a slush fund you can draw on for such things, but it's doubtful.

I also buy things like stickers because they make me happy. Oddly enough, it makes most students happy too, even if they're sixteen. It's something I use in my job but it's not like I can fill out an expense sheet and get reimbursed for that.

Source: https://www.pinterest.com/pin/266345765435635454/

Myth #17: Teachers in private schools couldn't get public school jobs.

As previously mentioned, jobs are out there, but not every available job fits a candidate's preference for commute, salary, and qualifications. I never expected to stay forever at the private school I worked in. To put it bluntly, they didn't pay enough. People do survive on low paychecks, but it takes a lot of dedication and sacrifice to work certain places.

I've worked in three public schools and one private school. I'm not exactly the picture of "stays put forever." Faith-based private schools usually require their teachers to hold to certain beliefs before they're allowed to complete the job applications. So, in a way, private schools are pickier than public schools. A public district literally cannot discriminate in most situations. They get to turn you away if you have a criminal record, but that's about it as long as you hold the necessary license.

People choose their job for many reasons. Public vs. private school simply becomes one more factor to weigh in the process.

Myth #18: Teachers get a lunch hour.

That's almost true at my current school, but that's because an hour-long lunch is what the students get as well. This is not the norm. In fact, I've never heard of another school with such a long lunch break. My last school had twenty-five minute lunches, and most schools have a half-hour.

Myth #19: Teachers don't have to go back

You don't have to do anything, but if you want to remain competitive, you should consider doing professional development and continuing education courses.

Myth #20: Teachers have lots of patience.

There's no way to escape the fact that your patience will be tested, but that's true of any career. Like most traits, you have as much as you need, and like a muscle, if you use it more, the trait will grow. It could just as easily be said that teachers have a lot of coping mechanisms that substitute for patience. You learn which battles to fight and which to let slide.

Everybody has their limits though, and running out of patience might be a big reason why a lot of people leave the profession. It doesn't necessarily have to be patience with the students. Parents, administration, copy machines, co-workers, and the daily commute could all be stressors.

I've drawn this list from two main sources:

https://www.eschoolnews.com/2011/08/05/ten-common-myths-about-teaching/
http://www.reallygoodstuff.com/community/21-myths-about-teaching/
If you go to the websites, you can find the original authors' responses to these myths. Sorry, I think I reordered them. It made sense to me at the time.

Chapter 4:
Every Job Switch was Good for Me

Introduction:

I want to share something I wrote down around the time I realized the first public school teaching job would not work out. I'll take out the names, but leave in the crappy grammar so you can keep the flow of the words. Please ignore the insane number of ellipses.

4/29/08:

I have to write everything that happened today up so I don't forget ... let's see wrote one referral because the child didn't show up for a detention. Gave one detention because the child threw a hissy fit when I wouldn't let her go to the bathroom that instant. Wrote another referral because another child threw a hissy fit because I wouldn't answer her question to her satisfaction ... she stormed out came back later and said the principal told her to come talk to me after class if she had a question ... but she said she wouldn't waste her time and said that's b*******. So, I had a nice list of things to write her up for. Also, I had another detention assigned for a boy who wrote WHORE on a girl's arm. Even though she told him to do so ... (I later found out) ... and had to write to the principal that a boy said he'd bring a bomb to school. I don't care what context it

was in, he was frustrated and wanted to blow off steam, idiot child can't say I'm going to bring a bomb ... not in these days.
Kid – "You're not coming back next year."
Me – mutters – "Of course not, I'm getting the h*** out of here."

4/30/08:
Same Kid moment
Kid comes into class and proceeds to unwrap a fresh piece of gum and stick it in her mouth, with slight exaggeration to let me know she's being a pain in the bum on purpose. As if I'm as slow as she is and wouldn't notice. After the customary, "Kid, spit out the gum, you know the rules ..." she pointedly ignored me ... finally when I did elicit a response it was "If you can ignore me, I'm going to ignore you."
"Kid, you have detention, what day is good for you."
She suggested some day after school, I suggested morning. I win. Friday morning 7:30, be there.
"I'm not coming in the morning."
"Yes, you are."

Later, "Kid, put the paper away."
No.
I take the paper away ... "You can collect this after class."
"I don't want it, you touched it."

Kids have been jerks this week. Basically, they're whining and whining about how much I'm NOT teaching them... when, the whining is the sort of wasting time that's preventing real teaching. It's a self-fulfilling prophecy, they keep making cracks about how this whole year has been a waste, so they're obviously not trying ... because they're not trying, they're not learning ... and they just can't see that the learning part has to be an active thing.

Today I got the complaint about the book assignments ... "We're just copying words" - um, completely missing the friggin' point of the homework.

Basically, I was not offered another job here at this school, so I'm taking that as a "this ain't for me" sort of thing. I've decided I don't really like children, they're whiny, self-centered little brats who think they deserve something for nothing and dislike the idea of work. Oh, I know I'm not good at teaching ... I'm not good at kid-handling or parent-babying. I won't suck up when someone's wrong and I won't always bow to the wishes of a 15-year-old ... I've no patience for stupidity, which is a chronic illness in a high school.

If I want to preserve my youthful beauty :-) I'm going to have to up and get out of the profession.

As usual, I am tired, but in addition, I'm hurt and confused. I don't know if I'm truly not good enough for this job or if circumstances conspired against me. Well-meaning people say not to take it personally, but that's very hard to do that when you have someone else saying "you're not good enough for us."

I've never failed at something so important in my whole life, and it's a painful and humbling experience. Part of me is just hurt at the lack of trust and direction.

Commentary:
What went wrong?
A lot. I've actually had to answer that question in subsequent interviews. I won't waste too much energy trying to dissect something almost ten years in the past, but it's worthwhile to do a quick analysis of what exactly didn't work out.

I discovered that having an appreciation for biology as a subject doesn't translate to enthusiastic biology students, especially when they're freshmen. That misconception was just my first-year naivety shining through. My school had a newly-minted science supervisor trying to help two brand new biology teachers. Just as success as a student doesn't guarantee success as a teacher, so

26

success as a teacher doesn't necessarily mean instant all-star supervisor. It's a learning process and skill that takes time to develop. Didn't know this then, but I really enjoy teaching chemistry more than biology. I can teach biology, but honestly, I find chemistry easier to convey. Neither is better or worse than the other, but chemistry relies a tad more on simple math concepts than biology. Over the years, I've also improved my classroom management skills.

Side note: Student teaching can be difficult too. I ended up in a suburban high school with three different mentor teachers, each giving different advice. While enlightening, that also made things terribly confusing.

Why the heck would I share that with you?
The stories and situations might change, but I think every teacher can relate to feeling that way at some point in their career. When you're pushed to the brink, you either pack it up and quit or give it another go and grow from the experience. Honestly, even though it would have made me miserable, I would probably have signed another contract with that school if they'd offered one simply because it was the familiar evil.

The unknown is scary but can often be wonderful. Every school switch has been for the better in some way.

Oh, and time has told me that while there are things I dislike about children (and humans on the whole), it's not them I dislike. I don't like their selfish attitudes, so I try to teach them a better way. I don't like when they whine, so I teach them to articulate what's really bothering them and how to deal with it. Sometimes, they just have to do things they don't particularly want to do. Life's like that, so they might as well get used to it early. I don't like their sense of entitlement, so I teach them to earn what they can and take pride in their accomplishments.

Side note: I let students know that I'm okay with a C if that's the best they can do. If they should easily be earning an A and they get a C, then I try to instill in them the desire to do their best. Not everybody's an A student, and I get that. But everybody's capable of some success.

Conclusion:
Why didn't I quit for good?
My life has worked on an open door/closed door principle. I'd tried sending out applications for other entry level biology jobs, but the first real opportunity that came along was the chemistry teaching position at my old high school. The timing turned out to be perfect. The private, Christian school I knew from the student perspective offered a safe place to explore a new subject and gain my confidence as a teacher.

I want to clarify that although this is the way it worked out for me, private schools should not be considered any easier to teach at. In many ways, they're harder to work for, but this isn't a contest in which job is harder. Every situation is unique regardless of setting due to the students you work with, the classes you're asked to teach, and the administrators running the school around you.

Moral of this Part of the Story:
Don't give up easily. Think long and hard about what you really want before choosing a path.

Chapter 5:
Step 1: Perspective: Why teaching?
Why You?

Introduction:
I'm going to throw a series of questions at you designed to help you define yourself as a teacher.

What brought you to teaching?
What's your story? Everybody has a series of choices and events that led them to becoming a teacher. My original reasons weren't particularly altruistic. I didn't want to go to medical school. I didn't want to do biology research, and I wanted to continue writing. I still loved biology, but the only logical career choice that hit all those check boxes was teaching. Since I had no official teaching background, I went straight for the Masters of Arts in Teaching program that would give me that experience along with the MA degree.

What currently attracts you to teaching?
Despite the self-doubts of the past, I'm good at what I do, and I enjoy working with teenagers. They possess an enthusiasm and vitality that's fun to be around. Everything is still a big deal, whether it's a chemistry test, a movie date, or the latest fashion.

Aside: I'm a fan of uniforms. Doubt the public school system will go for it here, but it does save on a lot of fashion angst.

What do you love about your job?
Every year is different. No matter how many times you teach something, there's always something new to learn about the subject, about people, or both. Each class picks up its own personality based on the mix of students you get. Some are quiet and polite. Some have a really tough time keeping quiet. Most have a decent mix of silly and serious students. It's refreshing to encounter variety.

What's unique about you?
Teachers are so focused on finding the talents in each student that sometimes we forget to look within. I'm a writer and a science teacher. I spend half my life thinking of murder mysteries and kids with special Gifts like telepathy, perfect empathy, and the ability to shape dreams. The other half of my life deals with chemistry, which involves the building blocks of life. I'm also adopted, which has greatly shaped my life.

What about your past or present has helped define you?
Your story will be different, but everything that's gone into shaping you will help you connect with your current and future students.

How can you use that experience to make the subject you teach come alive for your students?
I like to think that I apply the same level of creativity that goes into my books to teaching. Creating characters requires a certain way of thinking. Hopefully, it makes me better at understanding people. I mentioned earlier that sometimes teachers have to be a bit of a detective. While previously I was referring to analyzing

handwriting for papers without names, it also applies to motivation.

Motivation's the heart of what makes any person work. If you can connect with people, you can learn what moves them. If you can move them, you can get them to work with you. It's not about control. It's about connections.

How can you connect with your students?

This has to be natural. Students know if you fake interest in something. For example, I have a colleague who loves Pokémon Go. Horrible as it sounds, I'm too old for Pokémon. I missed the bandwagon by about five years. It's just not my thing. On the other hand, I'm a huge Star Wars fan. Last year, I did a six week countdown to Rogue One's release. The students didn't say much, but I know a few of them appreciated it.

Whether it's movies, music, books, or television shows, let pop culture form some natural connections between you and your students.

Your turn:

What brought you to teaching?

What currently attracts you to teaching?

What do you love about your job?

What would happen to the students you work with if you left suddenly?

What's unique about you?

What about your past or present has helped define you?

How can you use that experience to make the subject you teach come alive for your students?

How can you connect with your students?

Chapter 6:
Step 1: Perspective: School Spirit

Introduction:
Your outlook will flavor everything.

Is it just a job or a calling?
You know what? No matter what answer you give, you can still be a very good teacher and have a fulfilling career. That's probably not the response you expected from me. I'm from the background school of thought that one should always try 120% at whatever you do. I've got zip for statistics, but on the whole, I've found teachers to be highly motivated and deeply dedicated to what they do.

Yet for every glowing noble moment, there are times when you'll be embroiled in conflict over the silliest things. I distinctly remember complaining my first year of teaching that the frustrating moments I was having were over dumb things like the kids chewing gum in my lab instead of life and death situations. I thought that if I'd become a cop or an Emergency Medical Technician or an emergency room doctor, then the crises would have real meaning.

Over time, I've come to realize it's about perspective. I once heard a pastor named Tim Lucas relate a story about his son who was crying hysterically. The root cause of that madness turned out to be that the older sister had taken the kid's ball away. To that child, the worst thing in the world was the removal of the ball. If only life's problems stayed that small. I'm not exactly grateful for the small frustrations in my life, but I'm grateful when they are small. Life and death situations are so much more glamorous in movies and books. Real life is … messy. Parents divorce, grandparents die, teenage romances come and go, friendships are strained over misunderstandings, and state games are won and lost.

Like it or not, as a teacher a part of the job is to support the kids in your classroom and provide a safe learning environment. I think that's actually written into some job descriptions and teacher evaluation schemes. You can't control the crazy stuff that happens to the students outside your classroom, but when they step into your room, give them a structured environment where for forty minutes to an hour, nothing will blindside them.

Money isn't everything:
It certainly helps, but happiness matters too. Teaching can be frustrating, but it's also an emotionally rewarding career. There are always small moments to celebrate, such as a struggling kid earning a good grade on a quiz or somebody making a key play in an important game.

The vast majority of employers out there pay a livable wage. Somehow you make it work.

What good things happened this week?
You don't necessarily have to make a list, but if you're a list person and that would help, go for it.

Examples:
- lessons that work
- no wait at the copier
- completed lesson plans

- email from a past student
- a beautifully formatted test
- good news from a coworker
- peaceful day in a rowdy classroom
- that rare gem: a positive parent email
- a good deal on sharpie markers/ gel pens/ loose leaf paper (Is anybody else a sucker for school supplies?)

Tip: Cling to those small victories. That might sound cliché or dumb, but thinking of good things leaves less room to stress.

School Pride:

Schools have various ways of encouraging teachers and students to get into school spirit. There's usually some form of spirit week where the classes battle each other for points by wearing hats or college sweatshirts or a class color. My current school lets teachers dress in jeans every Friday if you pay $2.00 which gets donated to a charity. One of my former public schools lets teachers wear jeans as long as the shirt/sweatshirt was something with the school's logo on it. Conveniently, they sold lots of varieties at the school store.

Tip: Whether your school store has T-shirts, sweat shirts, and other apparel or not, wait until one of the sports teams is doing a fundraiser then buy from a kid in your class. The trick will be learning to say no. Buying directly from a kid can open up conversations about the sport they play.

Get Involved:

Don't go crazy here. Schools always have something going on. If you enjoy a certain activity or have a passion for a certain cause, see if your school has a club on it. If you can't find something, consider starting a club that fulfills the need. If you're thinking "I would but I don't have the time," then attend events that are already planned.

Find something you like to do. There are usually several sporting events each week. Teams typically have about half the games on the schedule at home. Most public schools have several sports running in a given season.

If sports really aren't your thing, then consider school plays or choir and band concerts. The students work hard at these extracurricular activities. They enjoy seeing that teachers go out of their way to see them perform.

Tip: Find out who coordinates chaperones for school plays and choir/band concerts. That way, you can attend and get paid to be there.

Tip: Make sure the kids know you saw them in action. Just work it into a casual conversation. Even a simple "hey, nice game last night" is enough to let them know.

Conclusion:

Although you should make time for school activities, you don't have to do anything that's not natural to you. Clubs and activities are always looking for extra free help, but don't feel obligated to get involved if you don't want to. Don't try to do everything. You'll simply burn out faster. Find the one or two things you have a passion for and share in the students' extracurricular trials and triumphs. Those are the moments they'll remember.

Chapter 7:
Step 2: Time Management: Lesson Planning

Introduction:

The schedule is simply something you're going to have to adjust your lesson plans to match. Schedules aren't something you have a great deal of control over unless you're on the school board and the district is considering other options. I've heard of block schedules with 80-minute blocks, which sounds entirely too long, but I've never actually worked under such a schedule before.

Planning is definitely within your sphere of influence.

Key Point: I like to keep things simple, so I'll tell you the golden rule of lesson planning: always over plan. Bored teenagers = bad situation.

Period Length:
Hour Periods:
Just right.

Forty to Forty-five Minute Periods:
It's like Goldie Locks. Forty-five minute periods are too short to run classes in much less work in lab time. Basically, a decent lab would take an entire period or spill over into the next day.

Fifty to Fifty-five Minute Periods with double period for lab:
Fifty minutes is fine. It's more than a normal period, but with college prep kids it was actually too long for lab classes. The last public school I worked in had double periods for labs, which would be nice for AP or honors classes, but it was hard to balance an extra fifteen minutes for the lunch period classes vs. the normal early or late classes.

Rotating Schedules:

The private school I was in did not rotate schedules, so period 1 was at 8:00 every day. I can't remember the schedule at my first public school, but the second one rotated days rather than periods. I believe the lab schedule controlled the six day cycle, so on a certain day you would have lab for first period. On that day, the students would stay for periods one and two. On the day that third period had their lab, they would come in early and stay periods two and three.

My current school has rotating periods, four in the morning and four in the afternoon on a four-day cycle. So A day, you see periods one to three and six to eight. B day, you see periods two to four and seven to nine. Whichever period is next to lunch will have their lab period. If it's a morning class, the students simply stay an extra twenty-five minutes. If it's an afternoon class, the students come in halfway through the lunch period.

The schedule looks really odd and takes quite a bit to get used to, but I like that you get to see the classes at different time periods. Many students come to school tired and wake up as the day goes on. With a rotating schedule, you see them at 8:00 one day, 9:00 the next day, and 10:00 the next day.

Planning for Forty-five Minute Classes:

I think aiming for two major activities or topics is enough to fill a forty-five minute session, but always over plan. It's way better to bump stuff to a subsequent day than to have twenty plus teenagers with nothing productive to do.

Planning for Hour-long Classes:

Kids need variety. So do teachers. With an hour to play with, usually three topics or activities can fit in the day. I usually have a five-minute Do Now that lets the students review previous lessons or gear up for the day while I take attendance and catch up those who missed class. Then, we move into our first activity.

Lesson Planning:

Since I don't know your content area, I can't help you plan actual lessons, but I can list some resources for you. There are places with pre-planned lessons you can buy, but I've never met a teacher who wasn't a control freak when it comes to their plans. Even when using somebody else's plan, it's natural to tinker.

If you happen to teach chemistry or biology, sign up for my Nonfiction 5 Steps newsletter, and I'll send you a free copy of *Biology and Chemistry Projects* you can swipe, modify, and use as you will. (Go to www.juliecgilbert.com for the signup link.)

Format:

Adjust according to your time needs.
5-10 minutes warmup/ Do Now
10-20 minutes new material
10-20 minutes reinforcement activity
5-10 minutes wrap-up/ Exit Ticket

While not every day can fit a plan like this, it's a decent format for introducing new material. Much as I hate to admit it, flexibility's essential because timing rarely works as envisioned on paper or a computer. The times you get a plan to work like clockwork are to be cherished. If you don't get to an Exit Ticket one day, it does become a nice Do Now for the next day.

Tip: No matter how often you give homework, try to not give homework on Fridays. The students will appreciate it, and you won't have to grade stuff Monday morning.

Tip: Where possible, I actually like quizzing on Fridays because it wraps up the week and gives me a chance to do the grading over the weekend. (If your weekends are so jam packed that you can't get any school work done then that doesn't matter. However, handing stuff back or at least having the grades ready to share by Monday makes you seem very efficient when in fact you've had three nights to spread the work out as needed.)

Resources:
Inclusion doesn't mean I necessarily endorse these sites or books. Most of them are search engines of a sort, so you'll have to do some legwork to make it useful. Also, be cautious and remember that some of these sites want you to buy the lessons.

https://www.youtube.com/ - contains a wide variety of videos. For best results, search by topic then watch a few of the results. You usually find something useful in the first few videos.

http://www.pbs.org/pov/educators/

https://www.sciencebuddies.org/

http://www.nea.org/tools/LessonPlans.html

http://www.nsta.org/publications/freebies.aspx

https://www.flinnsci.com/ - great place for finding videos with how to do specific demos.

Demo a Day: A Year of Chemical Demonstrations

Find a template that works for you:
Your school might have a set template they want you to use. I always make two versions of my lesson plans. One version has all the standards and objectives and so forth. This is the one that I turn in to the supervisor. The other version is a printable one that's stripped down to the actual lesson and the homework. That's the one I carry around with me on my clipboard. Some

people still do hand-written lesson plans. If that works for you and you're allowed to do that, go for it.

Since my school has a rotating four-day cycle, I've gone with simple boxes in a Word document. It's got three columns, one for categories and two for days and usually extends four to six pages for the full version.

Find a convenient time to work on plans:
Some of my colleagues work every spare moment of their prep periods and hall duties to get their lesson plans done mid-week. I never could concentrate well enough for this. For me, Saturday morning and afternoon and occasionally evening belongs to lesson planning. It takes me a little while to settle in, but then I can get a lot done. Sometimes family schedules dictate when you can and cannot work on lesson plans, so Saturday might not work for everybody.

Tip: I recommend only staying two to three weeks ahead because things change and plans have to be modified. You want to keep some room just in case things come up and you have to miss a few days. Be nice to your substitute teachers and leave them detailed plans.

Pace yourself:
Don't try to do everything at once for the entire year. Plan a week at a time or a unit at a time, whichever is more convenient for you.

Conclusion:
There's no real right or wrong way to plan your time, but switching activities allows for the students to exercise different parts of their minds.

Chapter 8:
Step 2: Time Management: Grading

Introduction:

Measuring progress is a large part of the job. That doesn't necessarily have to mean grading, but often, grading is involved. The trick is to make sure whatever amount of grading you set out for yourself, it's doable in a timely manner.

Grading Policies:

You need to develop a policy for late materials. I have one of the more lenient policies. I do take late work even really late work as long as I haven't handed it back yet. (Use your discretion for the occasional exception on an individual basis.)

I reserve the right to take 10% off the grade for every day it's late usually until the grade is just barely passing. Some teachers don't even take late work or only take it under extreme circumstances. I'm okay with policies like that, but they're difficult to enforce if the students are failing the class because of it. I like having a generous policy because then I can say to the parents that their son or daughter had every opportunity to make up the work and chose not to do so. That puts the onus on the student.

I like having a "no extra credit" policy. This past year, my department had such a policy in place. That was beautiful because it took some of the pressure off me. If it's left up to the individual teachers, then me sticking with a no extra credit policy becomes harder to stand by.

Assignment Extensions:

I weigh each case in light of the surrounding circumstances. Some are automatic and easy. If a student's absent unexpectedly for a long time, then they need to meet with me and schedule when they'll make up their missing work. If a student knows they'll be absent for a long time, then they're expected to meet with me before to schedule when they can make up work. If there's a family emergency of some sort, then the extension fits the length of the disruption. Some types of disruptions throw a kid off way longer than they're out of school, so if that's the case, I'll consider modifying the workload or working with a very generous extension.

Homework:

Most of my units have two to three homework sheets. I rarely grade them, but if I do grade them, I give the students plenty of advanced notice. This past year, I worked in several mixed in-class resource classrooms.

Lab Reports/ Essays/ Projects:

Science teachers get lab reports. English and social studies teachers get essays and book reports. Math teachers and others at least end up with projects to grade. At some point, there's usually a large stack of something that needs your approval.

I only had eleven students in my honors chemistry class this past year, but I still dreaded grading formal lab reports. If I had any more than that, I'd break it into sections. I made a point of only grading lab reports at school. Not everybody has that luxury.

Tip: Find a small canvas bag that holds about ten projects or lab reports. Use this to ferry small sections of the workload with you so it naturally breaks down into something more reasonable.

Tip: When designing a project, make sure there's an easy to use rubric. Most official rubrics aren't user friendly, but most can be modified. Also, don't be afraid to put the students into groups where appropriate. If you grade most of the project by group and have a small individual component, everybody has to get involved but the bulk can be graded in a fraction of the time you'd need if you graded a project for everybody.

Tip: Limit or ban the use of glitter in projects unless you want to be wearing it for months and finding it everywhere forever.

Informal Assessments:

Do Nows and Exit Tickets are naturally informal assessments. If I look at the assignment, I grade by checkmarks that don't count for or against a student's grade. Sometimes, I ask them to put the Do Now in their notes and go over the answer with them instead of collecting it. In either case, the students should be able to determine how well they're picking up on a topic. You can turn it into a weekly classwork grade if you wish, but that requires a lot more bookkeeping.

A current colleague of mine gives a Do Now quiz basically every day. He grades every single one. He's also the guy at the school until the evening several times a week. While you probably don't need to go to that extreme, he has a whole heap of data to back up the grades in his class.

Self-assessment:

Sometimes, I ask the students to check their own understanding by rating their level of comfort with a topic. They hold up a hand with one finger raised for the topic being super easy and five fingers for the topic being super hard. If most are at a one or two—and I believe they're being honest with themselves, we move on. And if fours and fives dominate the room, I try to explain it a different way or do more practice problems.

Quizzes/Tests/Other Formal Assessments:

I designed most quizzes to take a half-hour, so reviewing briefly then letting students have the rest of the period to finish a quiz typically gives them more than enough time. I allow the whole period for tests. Believe it or not, I'm one of those strange people who actually enjoys grading tests and quizzes. Knowing how well the students have retained the information fascinates me.

Tip: Have something for students to do after a quiz. Some will always finish early no matter how much time you give them.

Tip: Double check to make sure they've answered every question. You'll usually remember the list of two to three students who need that extra nudge to finish.

Extra Time:
I know this issue of extra time shows up in a lot of IEPs (Individualized Education Program) and 504 Plans (a US federal law concerning students with disabilities), but typically, it's not been a problem for me. I usually always grant students enough time as they want for a test or a quiz. If it becomes a habitual thing, I try to work out a plan where they get the test in stages so they don't have time to go away and study some more. In my experience, kids don't want to come back to finish up a test or a quiz.

Tip: I've also built in a lot of extra time to each test and quiz. Those who don't need the full time get a jump on their homework or the next lesson, while those who do simply have more homework.

Conclusion:

Don't make more work for yourself. You need enough grades to ensure that one poor test score won't kill their grade, but you also don't want to be grading every day.

Chapter 9:
Step 3: Working in Me Time

Introduction:
Relaxing helps keep one's sanity.

Define your stressors:
What do you worry about?
- Bills
- School
- Family illness
- Personal cause
- Personal illness
- World affairs
- Something else?

If something truly bothers you, it won't take you long to define what it is. Notice how most of these things lie beyond your control. So don't worry about them. Be aware of them. Deal with them in small, manageable steps, but try not to let them grab hold of your spirits. Don't try to do everything yourself. In addition to finding ways to deal with your problems yourself, turn to family and friends for support.

Brief soap box moment: I think American culture emphasizes personal strength to an unhealthy degree. Humans are social creatures. It took more than one of us to create the problems in the world, and it's going to take more than one of us to fix them. Things like "world affairs" can be completely crossed off your list of stressors, as can most things that lie outside our control. I'm not saying you shouldn't be passionate about causes, but find something tangible to fight for. World affairs can be broken down into a hundred different issues such as human trafficking, clean water, access to medicine, and hunger. Don't overwhelm yourself with things outside your sphere of influence.

Dealing with your stressors:
Baby steps. Break them into manageable chunks. School's actually a great stressor because many aspects of the classroom lie within your control. Life's about balance.

Family Time:
Too much time with family can be a stressor in certain situations, but if it's scarce enough, family time can be a great way to unwind and forget your problems for a short time. Whether it's a movie, a game night, or just a meal, spending time with your family's good for you. But remember it's a balancing act. If you have small kids and they've taken over your life, then find time to step away and concentrate on the other two main areas of time.

Friends Time:
I'm an introvert. Although I don't have many friends, the few I have are ones I cherish deeply. Since they're scattered all about, I hardly ever get to see them, but I write them emails or send text messages. Phones, like making phone calls, aren't really my thing, so chatting on the phone doesn't usually happen. I prefer having coffee or lunch or hanging out and catching up. These things work for me.

Do activities that are fun but low maintenance. Planning big trips is fine on occasion, but don't let spending time with friends become a stressor in your life.

Me Time:

People need varying amounts of alone time. I have the option to have as much or little of it as I want because I'm not married and I don't have kids. Writing takes a tremendous amount of time, but it's fun and relaxing to me. Taking walks, writing real letters, listening to audiobooks, reviewing things, and building Lego sets are other ways I pass time. I'm never bored. There's always a good book out there or one that needs proofreading.

Not everybody's in that position, but regardless of what position you're in, you need some me time. Some people require a great deal more of it than others, but I think it's especially important for teachers because much of the job deals directly with people. There's something therapeutic about spending some time alone with your own thoughts. Whether that happens in your car on the way to work or in the grocery store, me time's a mindset not necessarily something you strictly have to be sans people for. If everybody around you in a coffee shop's a stranger, then you're still essentially by yourself. Take the time to think, to reflect, to recover your wits.

Conclusion:

Balancing time with friends, family, and yourself will help you maintain a healthy mindset. Teaching's a pretty emotionally demanding job sometimes. From a certain point of view, you spend a good chunk of your week helping, guiding, and instructing people. That's a heck of a lot of people energy expenditure, so you need positive time alone to restore your private energy reserves. Even extroverts need some me time.

Chapter 10:
Step 4: Classroom Management

Introduction:

Classroom management's a skill learned best by doing, but there are a few things you can do to make your life easier. Some classes will run like a smooth machine while others will make you question your career choices. You need to learn to pick which battles you're going to fight.

The Root of the Problem:

It starts when they're young. There's a dangerous philosophy going around that children will be scarred by correction. For better or worse, daycare centers pop up all over the place like dandelions. I'm not saying daycares are necessarily bad, but they're a poor substitute for the type of parenting done in ages past. Legally, the workers aren't allowed to discipline children in most situations. Even timeout has fallen out of favor as it might be emotionally scarring. The result is much of a budding generation of kids who do what they want when they want with very little impulse control. Chaos.

Fast forward a few years and these wild toddlers enter the school system. In placing such a high emphasis on respect for self, American culture largely forgets respect for peers, teachers, and property. There are many good kids in every class, but mix in just a few who haven't learned basic principles of respect for others and you're in for an epic struggle.

Your Classroom is Your Kingdom:

It's not a democracy. It's a benevolent dictatorship, emphasis on the benevolent part. You either enjoy working with kids or you're completely nuts and in the wrong profession. While a vibrant, successful classroom could—and often should—be full of activity, order still needs to reign. I've read articles that say you should involve the students in deciding how the classroom should be run, and that's fine to a certain extent. You want them to be comfortable and feel involved, but ultimately, you need to decide ahead of time how things should happen. Everything from how and when to sharpen pencils to leaving to use the restroom needs a policy. It doesn't have to be written down, but the students should be aware of your expectations.

Tip: Hit reset. If things aren't working, don't be afraid to have a frank conversation with the class about what's working and what's not. Depending on their maturity level, you might get them to establish some boundaries and rules they'll follow. Do this with caution because you never know what they're going to say. It might be an enlightening conversation to have anyway.

Boundaries:

Besides feel-good community service sort of stories, the main time you hear teachers in the news is when somebody's gone and done something stupid, illegal, or both. Set boundaries for yourself and your students. It's great to be friendly but not always recommended to be friends with students. I'm friends with some former students, but that's different. The emphasis is on the word "former." People who have trouble establishing proper boundaries have a tough time coping with classroom management issues. The students will treat you with a different level of respect if you're striving to be their friend.

Know Their Names:

I'm actually fairly lousy at learning the students' names, so I've taken to having them create nameplates for me to use the first few weeks of class. Have the students fold a piece of white printer paper in half either long ways or short ways. That difference determines how much space you have. If you're only after the first name, then the short ways is fine. By that I mean it looks like a normal piece of paper in portrait mode, not landscape. Next, have the students fold the two sides so they meet the center crease just created. They should write their name on one of the sections closest to the crease. Finally, they should stand the name upright and turn it so that it faces you. I learned that trick during a demo lesson.

Handling Chatty Students:

Some students talk to everybody, including themselves if you stick them in a corner. When you can't silence them for long, you should at least harness the energy. While not always practical, it helps if you give these students special tasks or direct on-task questions to them.

Tip: The ones that can't stop talking usually like helping or at least doing something. They get bored easily. Involve them in as many ways as possible. Give them tasks like handing back folders or collecting and collating folders.

Folder System Aside: One of my former teachers got me into a folder system. I put all graded papers into a folder with their name and assigned number on them. The benefits of this are two-fold. First, you don't have to spend much class time handing back stuff because the students can just pick up their folder on the way in and leave it on the way out. Second, in assigning the students a folder number, you have a very simple system for alphabetizing your papers. Put the papers in numerical order and they're automatically in alphabetical order if the numbers were assigned that way.

Restroom Policy:

Pretty sure you can't stop students from using the restroom, but you can direct them to the best times for stepping out of class. I prefer the beginning of class while everybody's still settling in. I disapprove of students sitting in class for five minutes doing nothing, then having to go as soon as the lesson starts. My students quickly learn I disapprove of such behavior so they generally ask before class, which is fine by me. There were quite a few occasions before tests when I'd be like "if you have to pee, go now because I don't want you leaving mid-test."

Tip: Make leaving their cell phone on their desk part of the restroom policy. It's amazing how much less time it takes to go to the restroom when their precious phone's back in the classroom.

Phone Policy:

No phones allowed, unless I give express permission to look something up. You wouldn't believe how many kids suddenly have the urgent need to check their grade in the middle of my class. You get to know the phone zombies quickly enough. If you can work it into class, like during a review game, that's great, but otherwise, enforce the school's phone policy to the best of your ability. Schools have varying policies. My current school leaves it up to the teachers. I think you can turn a phone over to the office, but usually, I just have nine-time offenders put the phone on my desk until the end of class.

Gum/Food Policy:

This one's easy because the classroom doubles as the lab. No gum. No food. I let the students quickly finish up eating something outside the room if they ask permission, but otherwise, there shouldn't be food in the lab. When I'm covering other people's classes, as long as it's not too disruptive, I don't care what food they have in a non-science classroom. If it disturbs other people, I might ask them to finish up outside the room or put it away.

I once had a student lick the glass stir rod we'd used to make rock candy. That got him kicked out of class and talked to by the vice principal. I believe the science supervisor also wrote the parents a long email about the safety contract which they had signed along with their son. You might think that an overreaction, but as I told the vice principal, I needed to make the point that the kid did something dangerously stupid. The whole crux of why there's a "no food in the lab" policy in the first place is that we have no way of predicting what chemicals have been on those counters and how well they were cleaned up.

Depending on what you teach, you may not have to keep such a policy at all.

Tip: I emphasize the no gum part because it keeps the general rule fresh in the students' minds.

Throwing Things Policy:
I make a pretty big deal out of "don't throw things" because we have too much glassware hanging round the room to make that safe. Incidentally, I have had everything from a muffin to a football thrown across my room. But I made a big enough scene out of it that I believe both incidents were the only major ones in their respective years.

Random Annoying Fad Policy:
Every year there will be some new popular thing to do that every student will be trying. This past year featured bottle flipping and fidget spinners. Since I teach chemistry and the students are used to my "no throwing things" policy, it wasn't much of a stretch to crack down on the bottle flipping in the classroom. I just learned to ignore it in the lunchroom. As for fidget spinners, as long as they didn't make too much noise and the students could get their work done, I didn't fight them too hard. In most cases, the

spinners become the distraction instead of the focusing tool they were supposed to be.

Defacing Property:

As much as you watch them, you can't stop students from drawing stupid stuff on papers, desks, periodic tables, and lab benches. Usually, I just ignore whatever it is and quietly erase or clean the desk or lab bench. If it's just a piece of paper, I'll throw it away. Generally, the culprits are after attention or acting out of boredom. If I know the culprit, I ask them to clean up the mess. Most of the time, you don't know the kid's identity. For example, one of my colleagues and I came in after a weekend and found red marker scribbled over several desk drawers. There was nothing to do but test out various cleaning solutions on it. I don't mind drawing so much as carving. That's a tad harder to fix.

Hostile Students:

When you work with dozens of students every year you're bound to run across a few who are actively hostile. At the end of my first year, I had one boy run in like a coward and toss a note onto my desk. It was an unsigned rant about every perceived wrong I'd ever done to his class. I considered keeping it, but instead, I crumpled it up and tossed it in the garbage where it belonged.

Don't let hostile students get to you. They may or may not be upset with you personally. Some are just ticked off at the world. Be polite. Be as firm or gentle as the case requires. Try to involve the students, but if they resist, leave them alone and try again the next day. You want them to know they're welcome to be a part of the class at any time, but while they're in grumpy mode, let them be.

Enforcement:

The keys to any policy are clarity and consistency. In other words, the students need to know what they're allowed to do and what they're not allowed to do. You have to be proactive both about steering them towards what you'd like them to do and away from what you need them to avoid doing.

Justified or not, "It's not fair!" is going to be a very common phrase in any classroom where you try to enforce rules. The complaining student is likely going to point out two or three other kids doing something wrong. Gently but firmly remind this student that you can only deal with one thing at a time then address the others as well.

Nobody's perfect. There are bound to be situations where the kids "get away" with doing something they're not supposed to do. However, it's important that you consistently attempt to uphold the rules you've established. Pick something to focus on and address it every day.

Tip: The phones and gum/food are great focal points. Why? Because in the grand scheme of things, they're minor. If the students are focused on infractions such as sneaking a pretzel under their desk, they're less likely to be defacing school property or terrorizing their desk neighbors.

Bargains and Rewards:

Phones can be a powerful incentive if used properly. Problem is, they're usually not used properly in class. I've seen students sitting in the back just playing games. Kids on their phone have a certain terrible posture and phones glow under desks, so it's pretty obvious when they're trying to sneak peeks at their phones.

Tip: If you want to turn phones into a reward, let the students listen to music if they get to a certain part of the lesson or finish a set number of problems. I make it clear that they don't get to sit there choosing music, they get to turn it on, stuff it in their pocket, and listen through earbuds until the end of class. That's usually only ten minutes or so, but it works swell.

Find other small rewards that work with your personality. I'm a crazy Star Wars fan, so I buy lots of stickers. School just gives me an excuse to slap stickers on papers. Whenever a student earns an A on a test or a quiz, I give them a sticker. It's a silly little thing, but they'll let you know if you forget to put on a sticker when they earned it.

Pencils, eraser caps, and other small school supplies can also be rewards, but usually these are just things that make the classroom run smoothly. I buy a good supply of these sorts of things out of pocket. If you go at the right times of the year, it doesn't feel like you're spending a lot of money. I may not like shoe shopping, but school supplies are fun to buy. They're so colorful.

The Art of Asking:
Learn the art of asking:
People are more favorably inclined to do something if they feel they have a choice in the matter. Just yesterday, I watched a Youtube video where the head of Buckingham Palace explained how working with civilians differed from working with soldiers. He made the point that with civilians there's a different way of asking. "Would you mind …" or "Can you do me a favor and …" instead of "Do …"

Random aside: Kids are funny. For some reason, "do me a solid" was a popular way of asking for something once upon a time. I'm sure it'll return someday. Anyway, once I had a student ask, "Ms. G. do me a solid. I gotta go to the bathroom." For the record, those two phrases shouldn't be put near each other.

Tip: Try to call on everybody evenly or at random. Some kids get very self-conscious about offering answers. I know that's not always possible because you don't always have enough questions to go around. There are numerous tricks to making the calling on system random. Popsicle sticks with names or numbers works well. I've also heard of teachers who have the students answer on notecards then switch several times. Then, when they're called on, they're actually reading somebody else's answer. This takes some of the stress of being wrong off of them. I'm probably going to try that one soon for longer, written answers.

Teach the students the art of asking:
This applies to many things beyond the daily workings of each classroom. In the last chapter of my 5 Steps chemistry book, I put a section about how to email their teachers. I'll put that small section as an appendix so you can modify it as you wish or just swipe it and put it on your websites. It's super easy, but it's best to reinforce the social skill rather than assume they already know how to talk to adults. (Appendix I)

Conclusion:
Every single class period is different. You have to read the situation and make adjustments as you go. Cherish the sweet classes and plan for the boisterous ones. Active's not necessarily a bad thing, but every classroom should feel safe. If the students know the expectations and see the rules being addressed regularly, they're more likely to comply with directions. This becomes especially important in science classrooms because students need to learn to follow directions to the letter in lab situations.

And have fun. Kids are very refreshing. They're moody, goofy creatures with a charming energy to them. Show them you love what you do and some of that good cheer might get reflected back to you.

Chapter 11:
Step 5: Good Communication

Introduction:
Good communication will make your life exponentially easier.

Communicating with Administrators and Colleagues:
Administrators have agendas to promote every year. Collaboration seems to be a recurring theme with them. In any case, it's nice to hear what my colleagues are up to even if it's not exactly the same thing I'm doing. Sometimes, they'll do projects or labs I want to try.

Can't say there's a magic formula for working and communicating well with colleagues and administrators. Guess it's just the usual principles of getting along with people.
- Be polite.
- Be respectful.
- Be yourself.
- Be open to new ideas but don't modify everything you do to suit somebody else's style.

Teaching's difficult enough when you're comfortable with what you're doing, without the added pressure of trying to be someone else. That said, if enough people give you the same advice, look into implementing it.

In written communication, always double and triple check your work. It's a good habit to get into and vital for making the best impression on your bosses.

Good administrators will support you and help you be the best teacher you can be. Poor ones will try to change fundamental things about you. If you're not getting along with the administration, take some time to reflect about what the conflicts concern. Do they have concerns about your teaching style, your classroom management, or something else? Try to handle your classroom problems on your own, but don't be afraid to ask for help. Many administrators were once teachers, most of these will remember how they handled similar situations, and a few will even be able to share that knowledge with you.

Embrace the small talk.
Notice I didn't say perpetuate the gossip. There's always something to complain about, but if you happen to be in a casual conversation with an administrator, don't unload on them! That's what colleagues are for. Use the time to ask about their family or weekend plans. In short, get to know them a little. The more you know somebody, the easier working with and for them becomes.

Parent Emails:
This past year, I experimented with the idea of emailing the parents every weekend. It's a bit of a pain to set up the first time, but worth the effort. Most grading systems give you access to every parent's email address.

I've been told that you should send a parent email home every time a student's grade goes up by a letter grade or down by a letter grade. To be honest, that never worked for me. I found my own system.

In the weekly email, I'd tell the parents what we did, what I'm excited for, what's coming up soon, and any important reminders the students should be aware of. Some parents immediately made their kids read the emails while others refused to pass any messages along in order to teach their kid responsibility. Whichever camp they fell into, I think most appreciated the communication. I work with tenth graders mainly, so they're about fifteen or sixteen years old. The likelihood of parents getting a detailed report about goings on in their kids' chemistry class are next to nothing. This way, at least the parents know when major tests, projects, and labs come up in class.

Reasons I think this works:
- It opens up lines of communication that aren't adversarial. When you need to contact a parent for a negative reason or ask them to check up on something for you, there's a cooperative note already set to your communication.
- Most parents appreciate being kept up to date.

Tip: Update your grades. Then report that the grades are updated. Repeatedly remind parents to check the online grading system so there are no nasty, end-of-marking period surprises for anybody.

Important Tip: Use BCC! (blind carbon copy)

Class Website:
Many schools require every teacher to have a website. Sometimes, this is merely a place for your official email to be posted. If you're not instructed one way or another, double check their communication policies. Then, assuming nothing prohibits it, set up a class website where you can post announcements, homework assignments, extra practice sheets, study guide keys, policies, and useful video links.

Communication with Students:

The student version of the weekly letter had a different tone than the parent one. I'll post examples of each at the back for comparison. The student one tended to be more casual but usually covered the same information. I put in gentle reminders or less subtle kicks, which days they should show up prepped for lab, test averages, upcoming exciting stuff, and anything else that seemed relevant. (Appendix II)

How much time did it take to write all those letters?
This year, I taught honors chemistry and college prep enriched chemistry. That required two parent emails and two student letters as well as updating the homework for the week. On average, the emails took an hour to compose and send or post.

Aside from the weekly letter posted to the class website, I didn't reach out to students much in terms of individual communication. However, I always replied to them in a timely manner if they reached out to me.

Tip: If a student (or colleague) has been sick for a while or suffered a loss, reach out and send a check-up email. It doesn't have to be terribly long and can have some business in it, but mostly, this is about forging connections.

Conclusion:

Find some way to be proactive about your communication with parents and students. Talk to your colleagues. Exchange pleasantries with administrators. Chat with them in casual settings like the lunchroom. Teaching's a very people-centric job. There's no avoiding them, so you might as well make the most of every situation.

Chapter 12:
Questions to Consider before Quitting

Introduction:

These questions are in no particular order. I leave some comments near a few of them, but they're really meant for you to work through on your own. To that end, I'll provide a blank version of just the questions and a little space for you to answer in the paperback version. The ebook version will just have the list so you can copy-paste it elsewhere as you like.

How many times do you cry?

Every day, every week, every month, never? Seriously, first year is the worst for most people. It gets better.

What makes you cry?

Is it the administration, the parents, the students, the stress, or all of the above?

This is kind of an important question because it can help you decide whether you need to become immune to certain stressors, you're in the wrong school, or teaching's not for you.

What would cheer you up?

Don't knock the short-term mood fix. Ice cream, a good book, a sticker? On the other hand, be aware that short-term fixes can only do so much.

What supports do you have on your side?
Do they really understand you or your job?

Family and friends are important. Some people have good relationships with their families and some don't. You can't control the world. You can only control how you react to tough situations, and having strong supports can go a long way in getting you through hardships and heartaches.

What steps can you take to get better at what you do?

If something's not working, it's worth looking into fixing the problem instead of walking away. If you think you're perfect, you might just be in the wrong profession. Teaching requires a lot of personal growth.

What would your ideal school look like?

It's a useful exercise to define perfection and evaluate where and how your current situation differs.

What level of student would you like to teach?

Honors, advanced placement, college prep, lower level? This can make a big difference. I've taught most levels at this point. Honors students tend to have less behavior issues, but they're higher maintenance in the grading department. They also come with bigger egos and tend to take correction less gracefully. Expect to have to explain every half point you take off. College prep students are a mixed bag. You'll get some high fliers from other departments, like English if you teach science. On the whole, they're sillier but you'll also have to fight more "hand in your homework" and "yes, this does matter for your life" battles.

Do you have the opportunity to teach your desired level at this school?

What would you like to be making each year?

Chapter 13:
Public vs. Private Schools

Introduction:

I enjoyed my time at my old high school. It wasn't exactly relaxing, but I certainly learned a lot along the way. The one I worked at had a religious affiliation, so I can't speak to every type of private school. By the way, I'm told that this public vs. private terminology could get confusing if you're from the United Kingdom. There, Public Schools, are actually the private, fee-based ones and State Schools are the non-fee everyday schools.

Pros to Working at a Public School:

- There's more staff, so you can always find somebody to turn to when looking for a fresh lab idea or a fun project to try. If you have a content question, there's an actual person to talk to instead of having to rely on an internet source or a textbook.
- The pay scale is a lot higher. Please note that this varies widely. I walked away from a job offer because it was roughly ten thousand less than what I'd had in my other job and two preps instead of one. I think my new school has a slightly lower pay scale, but I entered at a slightly higher level, so the amount I made at each was nearly identical.

Cons to Working at a Public School:

- There's more staff, so you have to collaborate more and do things like common assessments.
- There's more staff, so there are more egos involved. More people. More problems.
- The class sizes are usually much bigger. The highest I ever had was twenty-six I believe, but most labs are legally designed to house twenty-four students. Some of my friends have had as much as thirty students in a class. Even with very big rooms, that's way too many students to have in a chemistry room. To be fair, I've also taught a public school class with as low as seventeen students in it.

Pros to Working at a Private School:

- There's less staff, so there's less need to make sure your lessons line up with anybody.
  I always chuckled when I got mail there because it was addressed to the "chemistry department" which consisted entirely of me.
- The class sizes tend to be smaller.
- The school tends to be smaller, so you know most of your colleagues and the student body.
- The parents generally support the staff on most issues.
- I could have a well-stocked candy drawer and hold class parties with food.

Cons to Working at a Private School:

- The pay scale is much lower than comparable positions in the public schools. (This statement may not be applicable to non-religious private schools.)
- There's less staff, so you have fewer people to turn to for fresh ideas about labs or lesson plans.

- Less staff means that if they want to offer a variety of classes, the teachers tend to get more preps. I have a friend who has something like seven preps each year. That's crazy. Granted, they don't all meet every day, so it's not like she needs to plan for five lessons every week for the classes. (I mentioned having taught 5th grade science. Here's where it happened. Don't get me wrong, I liked the students, but it was still strange to go from honors chemistry to 5th grade science and then back to chemistry students just because they couldn't hire another intermediate school teacher.)

Other Teaching Opportunities:

Please note: Inclusion in this list does not mean I endorse these organizations or lists. I'm just letting you know what's out there. Most job posting sites like Indeed.com will have listings if you're in the market for a job.

https://www.teachforamerica.org/
http://www.worldteach.org/
https://www.teachers-teachers.com/

The pH Scale:

The pH scale measures the power of the hydrogen ion you get in solution. If you have extra H^+ ions in solution, you will have an acid. If you have extra OH^- ions in solution, you will have a base. The scale itself runs from 0 to 14. The 0 side represents very strong acids. The 14 side represents very strong bases. 7 is neutral. The closer you get to 7, the weaker your acid or base will be.

Chapter 14:
Life Lessons to Teach Students

Introduction:

We live in an age where there's a ton of information out there. It's not solely about learning facts anymore. It's about interpreting them and using knowledge to create new solutions to old problems.

Honesty:

You may never know who cheats in your class. Kids are devilishly clever when they want to be. Oh, you'll catch the bad cheaters, but some will inevitably slip through. The teacher's role has changed over the years. Instilling a sense of honesty still rests mainly on parents, but teachers need to reinforce that life lesson every chance they can get.

How do you teach honesty?

You tell them right from wrong. Cheating isn't merely wrong for the sake of being wrong. It hurts them in the long run. The mind's a powerful thing. The students may or may not make the right choice in the moment, but they'll remember that lesson long afterwards.

Hard Work and Responsibility:
I try to let my students know that I expect the best from them. If they earn a B by trying their hardest, that's wonderful. If they earn a B but they could do better, then I want them to step up their effort.

Fact: You won't like everything you're asked to do in life. That does not translate into a right to do something with half your brain.

Responsibility and Tact:
It's perfectly acceptable to get involved in school plays and sports and clubs, but students need to remember that their first job is to do their best in their courses. I understand tech week just before a school play is crazy-stressful on the students in it, and I sometimes adjust things accordingly. But the world doesn't always shift to suit you, and the sooner kids learn that lesson, the better.

Kids are going to interact with you, and sometimes you need to gently but firmly let them know when they're doing it wrong. I've had to tell students that it's not a great idea to basically tell me that my class was last on their list of things to do so they'd like an extension on the project I assigned a week ago. How they present their requests can make all the difference.

Time Management:
Being a student requires time management. I don't envy kids having to learn five to six different teacher's quirks alongside the subjects. There's enough time for everything if one makes tough decisions. Students get involved with a lot, which is great, but sometimes they need to learn when and how to choose their priorities.

Grace and Good Will:

There will be countless opportunities when students will wittingly or unwittingly throw themselves upon your mercy. They'll ask for an extension on a project or to be allowed to hand in something late. You're going to have to walk the line between teaching responsibility and grace. Keep in mind that grace can sometimes earn good will.

When you decide in their favor, make it clear that they know it could have gone either way, but you're helping them out in this case. You want the student to understand that things won't always go their way and they shouldn't make a habit of needing to be helped in such a way.

Warning: Do not change grades arbitrarily. Individual projects or tests or quizzes have plenty of places for partial credit and if you want to re-evaluate your point distributions, fine. But be careful when granting grade changes. You do not want to put yourself in the position that parents and students feel free to request whatever grade they feel like they earned.

Common Sense:

Units are a big thing in chemistry, so I emphasize it on everything from classwork to homework to tests. Some people come wired with a lot of common sense, and others need more reminders. Ask students to always double check their answers and make sure it makes logical sense. One of my colleagues brings up paperclips and football fields. She once asked students how many paperclips could fit from one end of a football field to another. I think one group answered fifty.

Sifting Internet Information:

The internet has a lot of information. Not all of it is true or edifying, but there is plenty of good stuff to find no matter what you're looking for. Teach students how to recognize sites that tend to be more reputable than others. Send them to good sites.

Don't let them use a site that can be modified by anybody unless they're just using it to find a place they can cite as a primary source.

Tip: Invite students to contact you if they want a source evaluated. In most cases, few will take you up on it. If an overwhelming amount of people contact you, then send them to a blog or website where you can post some good and bad examples so you don't have to answer the same question a hundred times.

Conclusion:
The lessons that reach beyond the classroom will stick with students the longest. Take advantage of the opportunity to help shape the next generation into responsible adults.

Chapter 15:
Bonus: Love What You Do

Introduction:

I hope soul searching will lead you back to teaching and confirm your calling, but understand that moving on is okay too. You will always have the memories. The length of service doesn't matter, only the quality matters.

The Ones You Remember:

Unfortunately, most students tend to be memorable for all the wrong reasons. But every class has a few students who stick with you for good reasons. Enjoy the memories that bring you joy and discard the ones that hurt.

Who Will Remember You?

You work with multiple students each year. Depending on your workload, that number could soar into the hundreds easily. You may or may not remember everybody's name as the years move forward, but some of them will remember you.

What do you want to be remembered for?

Defining this ahead of time may help you shape what sort of teacher you want to be.

Teacher types: (not a comprehensive list; just a start)
- Lazy teacher – never returns anything, grades super slow
- Crazy teacher – totally unpredictable
- Tough teacher – frowns upon fun
- Tough but fair teacher – strict but fair
- Funny teacher – constantly amusing everybody
- Dumb teacher – doesn't know anything
- Clueless teacher – oblivious to the class
- Wise teacher – super smart
- Awesome teacher – cool and knowledgeable and fun

Timeless Lessons:

Some students are going to get your brand of humor and some won't. Work to create something memorable but don't forget the timeless lessons. Odds are good they won't retain much of the content, but if you can teach students how to learn, you'll help them along the journey to become better people.

Other timeless lessons:
- Be kind.
- Be honest.
- Be creative.
- Be yourself.
- Work hard in all that you do.
- Be proud of what you've earned, even if it's less than perfect.
- Life's a balance between beauty and disaster. How you deal with daily life will determine how you react to crisis.

Cling to the Good:

No matter how rough a year may be, there will always be good things to remember. As your career moves forward, you'll hear from or about former students. I make a point of asking each of my students what they plan on doing for a career. Some don't know, but others have a detailed plan already.

Although it makes one feel old, it's kind of cool to see what former students become. One young man said he'd be a food scientist, and he did just that. I received a nice letter from a young lady I taught a couple of years ago, saying she wanted to become a writer in part because of me.

Love What You Do:

People ask if I'll ever quit teaching and go write full time. To be honest, I don't know. I love doing both. There's a nice balance between having the beautiful order and chaos of a chemistry classroom seven hours a day, some nights, and most weekends for ten months, and then concentrating on writing for two months.

Most people innately know why they love teaching. There are many reasons. I'll list a few that resonate with me, but you're going to have to come up with the reasons that work for you.

Non-exhaustive list of reasons why teaching is awesome:
- Teenagers are fun to be around – they're sarcastic, moody, goofy, funny people just starting to discover who they really want to be
- Chemistry is awesome – the units build on one another and it's the central science
- Always learning new things – you really want to understand something, teach it
- I'm good at what I do
- Making a difference in untold ways
- Helping people in small ways every day
- Working with highly motivated, creative people

Conclusion:

If you can look back at the year and remember more positives than negatives, then I'd call it a success. It's a privilege to be part of so many people's lives, even if only for a short time. The world is as big or small as you make it. Instead of feeling like you have to take on the whole world, change the world of a few kids for the better.

The End

Appendix I:
How to Teach Students to Address Adults

How to Talk to (and Email) Adults (Specifically, Your Teacher):

- Be brief.
- Be clear.
- Be polite.
- Be you.

There are many reasons to contact your teacher(s). Sometimes, you need to inform your teacher(s) of a planned absence due to a field trip, a family vacation, or a death in the family. Sometimes, you need to ask about the details to a project or homework assignment. Check the class website first, but they're not always updated. Sometimes, you need to ask for an extension on an assignment due to extenuating circumstances. Maybe you want to know how you did on a test or need to get a grade changed because what the paper says is different than what the online system says. The scenarios are pretty much endless, but the four bullet points above are your best bet for obtaining the most favorable outcome of the situation.

By the time you're in chemistry, you're in high school. It's time for you to present your own requests. I'm not saying there aren't situations that warrant involving your parents, but they should not be your first go-to option. Any time you involve additional people, things get more complicated.

Mistakes happen. I've definitely entered grades wrong, and in those situations, I'm happy to fix the problem as swiftly as possible. If you've earned a grade, you deserve it to be reflected properly in the overall scores. That said, do not send requests to have a grade changed based on the reasoning that you "worked hard." Working hard is the expectation, and the grade earned will already reflect this. 89's do not magically turn into 90's because you're nice. If they did, the entire grading system would become arbitrary and meaningless.

When you compose an email to a teacher, you want to be clear and to the point as well as polite and respectful. Remember, if you're contacting your teacher, typically it's because you want something. People respond better to nice, polite emails. Part of being clear is stating who you are and possibly what period you're in. You may or may not get your way with the request, but you're more likely to get a favorable response with something clear, genuine, and polite. Always take a moment to double check the grammar too. It's just a good habit for corresponding with anybody in a formal setting.

Appendix II:
Sample of Weekly Parent and Student Emails

Honors Chemistry

3/25/17

Dear Parents,

The honors students just wrapped up the solutions unit. We ended with several labs, a review, and the test. The rock candy lab went decently, though only one batch came out actually forming the crystals as it should. The class average on the solutions test was 84%.

The marking period actually ends on April 5th. I thought it ended just after the break. If your son or daughter is missing any work, please have them turn in the late labs and homeworks very soon. April 5th is not this Wed, but it is the following one. No late work will be accepted after the close of the marking period.

Next up: kinetics and equilibrium. This is the study of the rate of reactions and the penchant for things to right themselves. I.e. As a reaction moves forward and uses up reactants, reactant concentration drops, so the rate of reaction slows.

Have a great weekend.

Sincerely,

J. Gilbert

Julie C. Gilbert

Weekly Letter 3/27-3/31/17

Hey,

Some of you are still having serious problems handing labs in on time. As we pointed out in class last week, we're running out of marking period here. All late work is due when the marking period closes on April 5th. That's a Wednesday. The class test average for solutions was 84.

This week, we're going to start Kinetics. We'll look at both kinetics and equilibrium before testing again, though you will have a quiz on the kinetics piece. You'll be working on a short project in class on Wednesday. Thurs, we'll talk about Rate Laws. Friday, we'll talk about equilibrium and do a minilab.

One of the rock candy solutions worked. You can see that in class on Monday.
Finish the marking period strong.

Sincerely,

J. Gilbert

Thank You For Reading

Each book—fiction or nonfiction—is a labor of love, and it's my pleasure to share the story or knowledge with you.

Please visit my website: http://www.juliecgilbert.com/ to find a link to the current free works. It is my goal that individual ebooks be free, but if you still wish to show support there are combination books and other formats such as audiobooks and paperbacks to invest in.

Search for "Julie C. Gilbert's Special Agents" on Facebook for monthly book discussions and giveaways.

I would love to connect with you. Please reach out to me via email at: devyaschildren@gmail.com or juliecgilbert5steps@gmail.com.

Other Contacts:
Facebook: https://www.facebook.com/JulieCGilbert2013
Instagram: https://www.instagram.com/juliecgilbert_writer/
Twitter: https://twitter.com/authorgilbert
Bookbub Partner link: https://www.bookbub.com/authors/julie-c-gilbert

Love Science Fiction or Mystery?

Choose your adventure!
Visit: http://www.juliecgilbert.com/

For details on getting free ebooks

www.ingramcontent.com/pod-product-compliance
Lightning Source LLC
Chambersburg PA
CBHW071833020426
42331CB00007B/1712